Healthy Cast Iron Recipes

Cast Iron Recipes That Are Healthy and Delicious!

BY: Valeria Ray

License Notes

Table of Contents

Introduction

If you are looking to eat a bit healthier but aren't sure how to do that with your cast iron, then this recipe book is for you! Filled with a wide variety of delicious dishes from breakfasts and sides to mains, the book has you covered!

What's more, all of the recipes in the book are easy to prepare and come with step by step, detailed instructions ensuring delicious dishes every time! So, what are you waiting for? Choose a recipe, take out your skillet and let's begin!

Baked Berry Oatmeal

Baked oatmeal is a wonderful breakfast—it's sweet, filling, and endlessly adaptable.

Makes: 4 servings

Prep: 5 mins

Cook: 45 mins

Ingredients:

- 2 cups rolled oats
- 1 cup fresh blueberries
- 1 cup fresh strawberries, halved
- ½ cup chopped pecans
- 1 tablespoon packed brown sugar
- 1 teaspoon baking powder
- 1 teaspoon ground cinnamon
- ½ teaspoon sea salt
- 2 eggs
- 1½ cups whole milk
- ¼ cup honey
- 3 tablespoons salted butter, melted

Directions:

Preheat the oven to 350°F.

In a large bowl, mix the oats, blueberries, strawberries, pecans, brown sugar, cinnamon, baking powder, and sea salt.

In a med. bowl, whisk the eggs, milk, honey, and butter. Fold the milk mixture into the oat mixture. Spoon the batter into the skillet.

Bake for 40-45 mins., or until crisp around the edges and cooked through. Serve hot.

SERVING TIP: Serve topped with crème fraîche or yogurt for a deliciously quick breakfast.

Skillet Fried Eggs

With a pat of butter (about 1 tablespoon) and a well-seasoned cast iron skillet, you're mere minutes away from the perfect fried egg.

Makes: 1 serving

Prep: 3 mins

Cook: 5-7 mins

Ingredients:

- 1 egg
- 1 tablespoon salted butter
- Pinch sea salt

Directions:

In the skillet over med-high heat, melt the butter.

Crack the egg into the skillet, on the hottest part of the skillet. Sprinkle the yolk with the sea salt.

Watch the egg carefully.

For an over-easy egg: When the white has cooked through, after about 4 minutes, flip the egg while the yolk is still liquid. Cook for 1 minute and serve.

For an over-medium egg: When the rim of the yolk has cooked through, after about 5 mins, flip the egg and cook for 1 min before serving.

For an over-well egg: When the yolk has almost completely cooked through, after about 6 mins, flip the egg and cook for 1 min and serve.

Potato & Rosemary Frittata

A frittata—somewhere between an omelet, a torta, and a quiche—is well suited to cooking in a cast iron skillet because the even distribution of heat in the oven cooks the eggs nicely.

Makes: 6 servings

Prep: 15 mins

Cook: 30 mins

Ingredients:

- 2 tablespoons salted butter
- 1 large red potato, thinly sliced
- ½ cup shredded Cheddar cheese
- 1 yellow onion, chopped
- 2 cloves garlic, minced
- 6 eggs
- 4 tablespoons water
- 2 tablespoons fresh rosemary leaves, chopped
- Pinch sea salt

Directions:

Preheat the oven to 350F.

In the skillet, melt butter over med heat. Add the potato, onion, and garlic, and cook for about 10 minutes, stirring occasionally, until the potato begins to soften. Spread the mix at the base of the skillet.

In a bowl, whisk the eggs, cheese, water, rosemary, and sea salt. Pour the egg over the potato mixture in the skillet. Cook for 3 to 5 minutes, or until the eggs begin to set. Transfer the skillet to the oven.

Bake for 12-15 mins. Slice in wedges and serve hot.

Brussels Sprouts in Olive Oil with Pistachios

This delicious recipe will delight even Brussel sprouts haters. The Brussels sprouts are blanched in salted water to keep them bright green, then finished with pistachios.

Makes: 4 servings

Prep: 5 mins

Cook: 5 mins

Ingredients:

- 1 pound Brussels sprouts, outer leaves removed, cored and quartered lengthwise
- Kosher salt
- ¼ cup (2 ounces) shelled pistachios
- 2 sprigs fresh thyme leaves, chopped
- 1 ½ tablespoons olive or vegetable oil
- Freshly ground black pepper

Directions:

Bring a large pan or a pot of salted water to a boil. Place the sprouts in & cook for 3 mins. Drain, rinse the sprouts using cold water, and then dry on a clean towel.

Add the oil, Brussels sprouts, pistachios, and thyme to a large cast-iron skillet and cook until heated through, turning often. Season to taste and then serve.

Slow Roasted Root Vegetables

Delicious root veggies with garlic and rosemary.

Makes: 6 servings

Prep: 10 mins

Cook: 75-90 mins

Ingredients:

- 1 bag baby carrots
- 2 onions, peeled and cut in wedges
- 3 parsnips, peeled and cut into thick slices
- 1 lb. baby red potatoes, washed
- 6 whole cloves garlic, peeled
- 3 tablespoons olive oil
- ½ teaspoon sea salt
- ½ teaspoon ground black pepper
- ¼ teaspoon dried rosemary

Directions:

In a 12" cast iron Dutch oven with feet, combine vegetables and garlic cloves. Drizzle with olive oil and mix to coat evenly. Add salt, pepper and rosemary. Gently mix together.

Arrange 4 hot coals in a circle and place Dutch oven over coals. Cover with flat lid and top with 6 more hot coals. Let roast for 75-90 minutes, adding fresh coals as needed.

Serve hot.

Seared Scallops

Almost nothing tastes better than a fresh scallop quickly seared in butter, so this recipe keeps it simple. Salt, butter, lemon juice, and a hot skillet.

Makes: 4 servings

Prep: 5 mins

Cook: 5 mins

Ingredients:

- 3 tablespoons salted butter
- 1 dozen sea scallops, rinsed and patted dry
- Pinch sea salt
- Juice 1 lemon

Directions:

Place a cast iron skillet over medium-high heat.

Add the butter to melt.

Place the scallops in the skillet. Sprinkle with sea salt and cook for 2 minutes. Flip and cook the other side for 2 minutes.

Remove the scallops from the heat, sprinkle with the lemon juice, and serve.

Blackened Red Drum

Drum is a firm fish with a moderate flavor and is particularly delicious when blackened.

Makes: 4 servings

Prep: 10 mins

Cook: 10 mins

Ingredients:

- 1 teaspoon ground chipotle chili pepper
- 1 teaspoon dried oregano
- 1 teaspoon freshly ground black pepper
- 1 teaspoon sea salt
- ½ teaspoon cayenne pepper
- ¼ teaspoon red pepper flakes
- 4 red drum fillets, skinned and boned
- 4 tablespoons salted butter, melted
- Juice 1 lemon

Directions:

In a bowl, stir together the chipotle pepper, oregano, black pepper, sea salt, cayenne pepper, and red pepper flakes. Set aside.

Place a dry cast iron skillet over medium-high heat.

Brush each fillet on both sides with melted butter and carefully coat both sides with the spice mixture.

Add the fillets to the hot skillet and cook for 2 to 3 minutes per side, until blackened and cooked through.

Drizzle with lemon juice and serve.

Shakshuka

Delicious eggs with tomato sauce and herbs.

Makes: 2 servings

Prep: 5 mins

Cook: 10 mins

Ingredients:

- ¼ cup extra virgin olive oil, divided
- ½ yellow onion, diced
- 1 jalapeño, minced
- 2 cloves garlic, minced
- 1 tablespoon (3.6 g) Aleppo pepper
- 1 teaspoon ground cumin
- 1½ cups (368 g) Tomato Sauce
- Kosher salt
- 4 eggs
- 3 tablespoons (3 g) minced cilantro
- 2 tablespoons (8 g) minced Italian parsley

Directions:

Preheat a cast iron skillet over med-low heat. Add 2 tablespoons (30 ml) of the olive oil and swirl to coat the inside of the skillet. Add the onion and sauté until soft, 4 to 5 minutes. Add the jalapeño and sauté until it begins to soften, about 1 minute. Add the garlic and stir through and then add the Aleppo pepper and cumin and stir through.

Add the tomato sauce, bring to a boil, and simmer until slightly thickened, 6 to 8 minutes. Season to taste with salt. Make four little wells & crack an egg into each one, and season each egg with salt.

Cover the skillet & simmer until the whites are nearly set and the yolks are still runny, 6 to 8 minutes. Top with the 2 tbsp of olive oil and then sprinkle with the cilantro and parsley.

Serve immediately.

Skillet Chicken with Sprouts and Apples from Brussels

Brown sugar and apples add sweetness to this skillet dish of chicken and Brussels sprouts.

Makes: 4 servings

Prep: 10 mins

Cook: 10 mins

Ingredients:

- 1 lb. chicken thighs, boneless and skinless
- 2 teaspoons new thyme, chopped
- Black pepper and kosher salt
- 1 tablespoon canola oil
- 1 box (12 ounces) shredded Brussels sprouts
- 1 apple, sliced
- ½ red onion, sliced
- 1 clove garlic, minced
- 2 tablespoons balsamic white vinegar
- 2 teaspoons brown sugar
- 1/3 cup toasted pecans, chopped

Directions:

The chicken thighs are seasoned with fresh thyme, kosher salt and black pepper. In a large skillet, cook in canola oil over medium-high heat until cooked through, 4 to 5 minutes on each side; move to a plate.

To the skillet, add the Brussels sprouts, onion, apple, & garlic clove. Cook for 5 mins, tossing, until the Brussels sprouts are wilted and the onion is softened. Stir in the brown sugar & white balsamic vinegar. Using kosher salt and black pepper to season.

Put the chicken back in, and top it with toasted pecans.

Serve.

Crispy Chicken with Smoky Chickpeas

Warm up with this quick but hearty weeknight recipe.

Makes: 6 servings

Prep: 10 mins

Cook: 25 mins

Ingredients:

- 3 teaspoons canola oil
- 8 thin bone-in, skin-on chicken thighs
- ½ onion, medium-sized, chopped
- 3 cloves garlic, chopped
- 1 ½ teaspoons paprika, smoked
- ½ teaspoon ground cumin
- 1 pint grape tomatoes
- 2 cans (15 ounces) chickpeas, rinsed
- For serving, new thyme leaves
- Kosher salt and black pepper, freshly ground
- ½ cup plain Greece yogurt

Directions:

Preheat the oven to 425 degrees F. Heat oil over med-high heat in an ovenproof skillet. Season the chicken with pepper and salt. Cook until skin is browned and crispy, 8 to 10 minutes, in batches, skin side down. Place the chicken aside on a plate; reserve the skillet.

Add the onion and garlic to the reserved skillet and cook for 2 to 4 minutes, stirring occasionally, until it begins to soften. Stir in the paprika & cumin & cook for 30 secs, mixing, till fragrant. Stir in the chickpeas & tomatoes, & bring to a boil. With salt and pepper, season. Nestle chicken in a mixture, side up on the skin.

Roast in the oven for 20-25 mins.

Serve with new thyme leaves and yogurt sprinkled alongside.

Mediterranean Frittata

A delicious frittata recipe with Mediterranean flavors.

Makes: 2 servings

Prep: 12 mins

Cook: 5 mins

Ingredients:

- 3 eggs
- ¼ cup feta cheese, crumbled
- 2 tablespoons pitted Kalamata olives
- ¼ teaspoon oregano
- ½ cup milk
- Salt and pepper to taste
- 2 cherry tomatoes, halved
- 1 ½ tablespoons olive oil

Directions:

Crack the eggs and beat with milk in a bowl. Season with the oregano, salt, and pepper.

Grease the iron skillet and heat on medium heat.

Add the egg mixture. Fold the edges of the frittata with a spatula and cook the eggs halfway through.

Add the crumbled feta cheese and sliced tomatoes on top and pop the skillet in the oven. Cook at 380F for 5 to 6 minutes.

Cool, slice, and serve.

Sweet Potato and Egg Hash

A quick and easy breakfast recipe with sweet potatoes and eggs.

Makes: 2 servings

Prep: 5 mins

Cook: 10 mins

Ingredients:

- 1 large sweet potato, cut into cubes
- ½ cup fresh spinach leaves
- 2 eggs
- ½ teaspoon cinnamon
- ½ teaspoon garlic powder
- 2 tablespoons oil
- Salt and pepper to taste

Directions:

Grease the skillet with oil & add the sweet potato cubes. Season with the cinnamon and garlic powder and sauté for 3 minutes.

Add the spinach & cook for 1 min more.

Crack the eggs on top and season with salt and pepper. Cover with a lid for 2 minutes to cook the eggs.

Serve.

Italian Egg Skillet

A flavorful egg recipe with spinach and mushrooms.

Makes: 2 servings

Prep: 5 mins

Cook: 5 mins

Ingredients:

- ½ tablespoon butter
- ½ cup mushrooms, sliced
- 3 cups raw baby spinach
- ¾ cup marinara sauce
- 4 eggs
- 2 tablespoons Mozzarella cheese, shredded
- Salt and pepper to taste

Directions:

Melt the butter in the skillet. Add mushrooms and cook for 5 minutes.

Add the spinach & cook for 1 minute.

Stir in marinara sauce and mix to combine.

Crack eggs evenly over the top of the vegetables and cover with a lid. Cook until egg whites are set.

Remove the lid and sprinkle with cheese, salt, and pepper. Serve.

Butter Herbed Rice

Herbed rice with garlic salt.

Makes: 2 servings

Prep: 5 mins

Cook: 5 mins

Ingredients:

- 1 1/8 cups vegetable stock
- 1 cup instant white rice
- 1/2 tablespoon dried parsley
- 1/2 teaspoon dehydrated chives
- 1/2 teaspoon garlic salt
- 1/2 tablespoon unsalted butter
- Salt and pepper to taste

Directions:

Preheat the skillet for 2 minutes.

Put the vegetable stock, rice, parsley, chives, and garlic salt in the pan and mix.

Cook for 5 to 7 minutes, or until the mixture starts to boil.

Remove from the heat & add the butter, cover and let it sit for 5 minutes.

Remove the lid, stir & season with salt and pepper. Serve.

Garlic Spaghetti Squash

A warm squash recipe with garlic and butter.

Makes: 2 servings

Prep: 5 mins

Cook: 5 mins

Ingredients:

- 2 cups water
- 2 pounds spaghetti squash
- 1 ½ tablespoons unsalted butter
- ½ teaspoon garlic salt
- Freshly ground black pepper to taste

Directions:

Preheat the skillet for 2 minutes. Pour in 2 cups of water, so you have ½ inch on the bottom of the pan. Bring the water to a simmer.

Cut the squash in half & place it in the pan, cut-side down.

Cook for 20 to 40 minutes, adding more water if necessary.

Remove from the heat & cool for 5 mins.

When cool, scrape out strands of the squash into a bowl.

Mix the butter and garlic salt with the squash. Add pepper to taste. Serve.

Roasted Brussel Sprouts

Sprouts with garlic and pine nuts.

Makes: 2 servings

Prep: 5 mins

Cook: 20 mins

Ingredients:

- ½ pound Brussel sprouts, trimmed, tough outer parts removed
- 1 ½ cloves garlic, minced
- ½ teaspoon cider vinegar
- 1 ½ tablespoons olive oil
- Salt and pepper to taste
- 2 tablespoons pine nuts, toasted

Directions:

Preheat the oven to 350F.

Heat oil in the skillet. Place Brussel sprouts in the skillet and cook until brown. Add garlic, vinegar, oil, salt, and pepper.

Put skillet in the oven & cook for 20 mins. Shake the skillet several times to ensure sprouts are not burning.

Remove from the oven. Sprinkle with toasted nuts and serve.

Curried Acorn Squash with Rice

Squash with curry and chickpeas.

Makes: 2 servings

Prep: 10 mins

Cook: 40 mins

Ingredients:

- 1 tablespoon olive oil
- 1 clove garlic, minced
- 1 small onion, diced
- 1 ½ cups acorn squash, peeled and cubed
- 1 tablespoon curry powder
- Salt and pepper to taste
- ½ cup brown rice
- 2 medium tomatoes, chopped
- ½ cup chickpeas, drained and rinsed
- ½ cup coconut milk
- 1 tablespoon tomato paste
- 1 cup vegetable broth

Directions:

Heat the skillet over medium heat. Add oil, garlic, and onion and cook for 4 to 5 minutes. Add squash and cook for 5 to 6 minutes. Add curry powder, salt, pepper, and rice into skillet and mix.

Add tomatoes, chickpeas, coconut milk, and tomato paste to skillet and mix. Cook until tomatoes start to break apart.

Pour in broth & bring to a boil. Lower heat and continue to simmer until liquid reduces. Continue to cook till most of the liquid is absorbed by the rice and rice is tender, about 40 45 minutes. Serve.

Garlicky-Lemon Zucchini

A quick and easy vegetarian dish with lemon and garlic.

Makes: 2 servings

Prep: 5 mins

Cook: 5 mins

Ingredients:

- 4 small green zucchinis, sliced about ¼-inch thick
- 1 ½ tablespoons extra virgin olive oil
- 1 tablespoon garlic, minced
- Coarse salt and black pepper to taste
- ½ teaspoon thyme, minced
- ½ lemon

Directions:

Heat the oil in the skillet for 1 minute.

Season the zucchini with salt and pepper. Cook in the pan until nicely browned on both sides, about 3 minutes per side.

Add garlic and cook for 1 minute. Sprinkle with thyme and salt.

Remove from pan and drizzle with lemon juice. Serve.

Ginger Kabocha Squash

Squash with maple syrup and ginger.

Makes: 2 servings

Prep: 5 mins

Cook: 10 mins

Ingredients:

- 1 tablespoon oil
- ½ inch ginger, chopped
- Salt and pepper to taste
- 1 teaspoon maple syrup
- ½ kabocha squash, peeled, seeded, and chopped

Directions:

Preheat the oven to 400F.

Heat oil in the skillet and add garlic. Cook for 2 minutes.

Toss squash in a bowl with salt, pepper, and maple syrup. Add squash to the skillet and cook for 2 minutes per side.

Cover skillet and place in the oven until squash cooks through, about 5 to 10 minutes.

Serve.

Open-Faced Egg Sandwiches

A healthy and filling breakfast or lunch recipe.

Makes: 2 servings

Prep: 5 mins

Cook: 10 mins

Ingredients:

- 4 egg whites
- 2 eggs
- 2 tablespoons grated Parmesan cheese
- 2 teaspoons butter, softened
- 1/8 teaspoon pepper
- 1/8 teaspoon dried rosemary, crushed
- 2 slices whole-wheat bread, toasted

Directions:

Coat a skillet with some spray & heat over med heat.

Whisk the eggs, egg whites, and cheese. Then, add to the skillet & cook till set.

Spread butter on 1 side of toast. Add the egg mixture on top. Garnish with pepper and rosemary. Serve.

Skillet Red Potatoes

A delicious side dish recipe.

Makes: 2 servings

Prep: 5 mins

Cook: 15 mins

Ingredients:

- 2 medium red potatoes, cooked & cut into 1/2-inch chunks
- 2 tablespoons oil
- 1/2 teaspoon dried parsley flakes
- ½ teaspoon garlic powder
- ½ teaspoon onion powder
- ½ teaspoon paprika

Directions:

Heat oil in the skillet. Add potatoes and cook for 10 minutes.

Stir in the rest of the ingredients. Cook for 5 minutes more. Serve.

Thai-Style Green Beans

Green beans with Thai flavors.

Makes: 2 servings

Prep: 5 mins

Cook: 5 mins

Ingredients:

- 1 tablespoon reduced-sodium soy sauce
- 1 tablespoon hoisin sauce
- 1 tablespoon creamy peanut butter
- 1/8 teaspoon crushed red pepper flakes
- 1 tablespoon chopped shallot
- 1 teaspoon minced fresh ginger root
- 1 tablespoon canola oil
- ½ pound fresh green beans, trimmed
- Chopped dry roasted peanuts and minced fresh cilantro (for garnish)

Directions:

In a bowl, combine the red pepper flakes, peanut butter, hoisin sauce, and soy sauce. Set aside.

In a skillet, cook ginger and shallot in oil for 2 minutes. Add green beans & cook for 3 mins.

Add sauce mixture and mix. Sprinkle with peanuts and cilantro and serve.

Ground Beef and Brussels Sprouts

Beef with cayenne pepper and Brussels sprouts.

Makes: 2 servings

Prep: 5 mins

Cook: 10 mins

Ingredients:

- ½ lb. ground beef (80% lean-20% fat)
- 6 ounces Brussels sprouts
- ½ tablespoon chili oil
- ½ teaspoon cayenne pepper
- ¼ teaspoon black pepper
- ½ tablespoon grapeseed oil
- Salt to taste

Directions:

Heat both the oils in the skillet. Add ground beef and spices. Cook for 7 to 8 mins/until the meat has turned dark brown. Stir occasionally.

Meanwhile, microwave the Brussels sprouts in water for 3 minutes on high heat. Drain and set aside.

Add the Brussels sprouts in the skillet with the beef and season with salt.

Cover with the lid and cook for 5 minutes.

Serve.

Flank Steak with Crushed Grapes

Meaty and fruity, this is a delicious dinner recipe.

Makes: 2 servings

Prep: 30 mins

Cook: 15 mins

Ingredients:

- ½ piece flank steak
- ½ shallot, chopped
- ½ clove large garlic, minced
- 1 tablespoon fresh rosemary, chopped
- 1 cup assorted grapes, seeded and crushed
- 1 tablespoon balsamic vinegar
- 1 tablespoon olive oil
- Salt and pepper to taste

Directions:

Combine the oil, balsamic vinegar, and herbs. Season with salt and pepper.

Rub the flank steak with this mixture and marinate in the fridge for 30 minutes.

Heat oil in the skillet and sauté the shallot with the grapes for 5 to 6 minutes. Remove from the skillet & set aside in a serving bowl.

Add the flank steak and cook for 4 minutes on each side, for medium doneness.

Remove and rest for 5 minutes. Then, cut into strips.

Serve with crushed grapes.

Cheesy Stuffed Peppers

Delicious peppers with beef and cheese.

Makes: 2 servings

Prep: 5 mins

Cook: 10 mins

Ingredients:

- 1/3 pound ground beef, lean
- 1/9 cup white onion, chopped
- 1 clove garlic, minced
- 5 ounces canned roasted tomatoes
- ¼ cup long-grain white rice, uncooked
- 2/3 cup beef broth
- 2/3 tablespoon tomato paste
- 1/6 teaspoon dried basil
- ½ cup cheddar cheese
- 1/3 tablespoon vegetable oil
- Salt and pepper to taste

Directions:

Heat oil in the skillet & add the white onion. Cook for 2 minutes and add the beef. Cook until brown and season with spices, salt, and pepper.

Add in the green pepper & garlic and sauté for 2 minutes more.

Add the beef broth, rice, tomato paste, and roasted tomatoes to the skillet. Reduce the heat & cook with the lid for 15 to 18 minutes.

Top with cheddar and cover with the lid. Cook for 2 minutes. Serve.

Turkey Fillets with Vegetables

This recipe makes for a healthy and fancy meal.

Makes: 2 servings

Prep: 5 mins

Cook: 5 mins

Ingredients:

- 1 tablespoon olive oil
- 3 anchovy fillets
- 2 turkey fillets, 4–6 ounces each, pounded thin
- 1/8 cup chicken broth
- ½ tablespoon capers, chopped
- 1 tablespoon dill, chopped

Directions:

Heat oil in the skillet. Add the anchovies and cook for 5 minutes.

Place turkey fillets and cook for 3 minutes on each side. Remove cooked fillets to a plate.

Add the broth to the pan & deglaze the pan. Stir in the capers and cook for 1 minute.

Pour the sauce over the turkey fillets and sprinkle them with chopped dill. Serve.

Sunday Roast Chicken

Cook this up every Sunday for a filling and healthy meal.

Makes: 2 servings

Prep: 10 mins

Cook: 30 mins

Ingredients:

- 1 small Rock Cornish game hen
- Salt and pepper to taste
- Small handful fresh oregano, tarragon, or thyme leaves, minced
- 1 ½ tablespoons softened butter
- ½ shallot, minced
- 1/8 cup stock

Directions:

Preheat the oven to 400F. Place 2 cast iron skillet in the middle rack of the oven.

Rinse the hen. Cut the spine off, then snip the breastbone to permit the bird to flatten. Pat dry the bird and sprinkle both sides with salt and pepper.

Mix the minced herbs into the softened butter. Slide your fingers between the skin and the meat of the chicken. Rub the butter under the skin and on top of the bird.

Remove the bottom skillet from the oven and place the bird, skin side down. Cook over med-high heat for 3-4 mins. Flip and place in the middle of the oven with the other skillet on top. Cook for 25 minutes, or until the bird reaches 160F. Place the bird on a plate and cover loosely with foil. Set aside to rest.

Place the skillet (that cooked the chicken) over medium heat. Heat until most of the liquid boil off. Then add the shallot and cook for 3 minutes more. Add the stock to the skillet & stir vigorously. Once the liquid has evaporated, turn off the heat.

Cut chicken in half. Serve with shallot and pan sauce.

Southwest Chicken Wrap

A filling and delicious wrap with beans and cheese.

Makes: 2 servings

Prep: 10 mins

Cook: 15 mins

Ingredients:

- ½ tablespoon olive oil
- 1 pound chicken breasts, cut into strips
- ½ yellow onion, sliced
- 1 teaspoon minced garlic
- ½ teaspoon taco seasoning
- 7 ounces canned black beans, drained and rinsed
- 7 ounces canned corn
- 7 ounces salsa
- Salt and pepper to taste
- 2 (12 inches) flour tortillas
- Shredded lettuce
- ½ cup shredded Cheddar cheese/Mexican-style cheese blend
- Sour cream to taste

Directions:

Heat oil in the skillet until hot.

Add the chicken & cook for 5 mins/till it starts to brown.

Add the onion and cook until the chicken is cooked through, about 8 to 12 minutes more.

Add the garlic, taco seasoning, black beans, corn, and salsa. Simmer until cooked through. Season with salt and pepper.

Remove from the heat. Spoon over the tortillas and top each with lettuce, cheese, and sour cream. Serve.

Chicken Fajita Wrap

A chicken fajita wrap with bell peppers and salsa.

Makes: 2 servings

Prep: 5 mins

Cook: 20 mins

Ingredients:

- 1 tablespoon olive oil
- 2/3 pound chicken breasts, cut into strips
- 1/3 yellow onion, sliced
- 1/3 yellow bell pepper
- 2 (12 inches) tortillas
- 1/3 teaspoon garlic powder
- 1/6 teaspoon onion powder
- 1/3 teaspoon paprika
- 1/3 green bell pepper
- 1/6 teaspoon cayenne pepper
- 1/3 teaspoon ground cumin
- Red pepper flakes to taste
- 1/3 teaspoon sugar
- 2/3 cup Mexican-style cheese blend
- Salsa and sour cream to taste

Directions:

Heat the oil in the skillet.

Add the chicken & cook until it starts to brown. Add the onion and bell peppers and cook for 7 to 10 minutes, or until the veggies are done, and the chicken is cooked through.

Toast the tortillas directly on the grill grate for 2 to 3 minutes on each side.

Add the garlic powder, paprika, cayenne, onion powder, cumin, red pepper flakes, and sugar to the chicken & cook, for 3-5 mins more or until well combined.

Remove from the heat. Divide the chicken mixture evenly among the tortillas and top with cheese, salsa, and sour cream. Serve.

Chicken and Zucchini Couscous

A veggie-filled meal with couscous.

Makes: 2 servings

Prep: 10 mins

Cook: 30 mins

Ingredients:

- 1 tablespoon olive oil
- ½ pound chicken, diced
- ¼ yellow onion, diced
- ½ tablespoon minced garlic
- ½ carrot, sliced
- ½ small green zucchini, cubed
- ½ small yellow squash, cubed
- 4 cherry tomatoes
- ½ cup chicken broth
- ¾ cup instant couscous
- ½ teaspoon ground cumin
- ½ teaspoon ground cinnamon
- ¼ teaspoon turmeric
- ¾ teaspoon seasoning salt
- Salt and pepper to taste

Directions:

Heat the oil in the skillet.

Add chicken and cook for 5 to 10 minutes, or until browned.

Add the onion and cook for 3 to 5 minutes.

Stir in the garlic, carrot, zucchini, squash, and cherry tomatoes. Cook for 5 to 10 mins/until the vegetables start to soften.

Add the broth, couscous, cumin, cinnamon, turmeric, and seasoning salt and mix well. Move to low heat.

Cook for 3-5 mins/until the mixture starts to boil. Cover and remove from the heat.

Let it sit for 5 mins. Add salt & pepper to taste and serve hot.

Conclusion

There you have it! Delicious recipes for you to make in your cast iron that are as good as they are healthy! Make sure to try out all of the recipes in this book, and if you like them, share them with your friends & family!

About the Author

A native of Indianapolis, Indiana, Valeria Ray found her passion for cooking while she was studying English Literature at Oakland City University. She decided to try a cooking course with her friends and the experience changed her forever. She enrolled at the Art Institute of Indiana which offered extensive courses in the culinary Arts. Once Ray dipped her toe in the cooking world, she never looked back.

When Valeria graduated, she worked in French restaurants in the Indianapolis area until she became the head chef at one of the 5-star establishments in the area. Valeria's attention to taste and visual detail caught the eye of a local business person who expressed an interest in publishing her recipes. Valeria began her secondary career authoring cookbooks and e-books which she tackled with as much talent and gusto as her first career. Her passion for food leaps off the page of her books which have colourful anecdotes and stunning pictures of dishes she has prepared herself.

Valeria Ray lives in Indianapolis with her husband of 15 years, Tom, her daughter, Isobel and their loveable Golden Retriever, Goldy. Valeria enjoys cooking special dishes in her large, comfortable kitchen where the family gets involved in preparing meals. This successful, dynamic chef is an inspiration to culinary students and novice cooks everywhere.

••••••••• ● ● ● ● ●•••••••

Author's Afterthoughts

Thank you for Purchasing my book and taking the time to read it from front to back. I am always grateful when a reader chooses my work and I hope you enjoyed it!

With the vast selection available online, I am touched that you chose to be purchasing my work and take valuable time out of your life to read it. My hope is that you feel you made the right decision.

I very much would like to know what you thought of the book. Please take the time to write an honest and informative review on Amazon.com. Your experience and opinions will be of great benefit to me and those readers looking to make an informed choice.

With much thanks,

Valeria Ray

Made in the USA
Las Vegas, NV
22 September 2024

95646628R00039